To the CORE...

Lisa Trumbauer

Raintree

Chicago, Illinois

Designed by Bridge Creative Services.
Picture research by Hannah Taylor and Rebecca
Sodergren.
Printed and bound in China by WKT Company
Limited.

11 10 09 08 07
10 9 8 7 6 5 4 3 2 1

**Library of Congress Cataloging-in-
Publication Data**
Trumbauer, Lisa, 1963-
  To the core : Earth's structure / Lisa Trumbauer.
     p. cm.
  Includes bibliographical references and index.
  ISBN-13: 978-1-4109-2577-0 (library binding-
hardcover)
  ISBN-10: 1-4109-2577-3 (library binding-hardcover)
  ISBN-13: 978-1-4109-2606-7 (pbk.)
  ISBN-10: 1-4109-2606-0 (pbk.)
 1. Earth--Internal structure--Juvenile literature. I.
Title.
  QE509.T78 2006
  551.1--dc22

                                    2006007583

Acknowledgments
The author and publisher are grateful to the
following for permission to reproduce copyright
material: 4 Corners Picture Library/SIME pp. **6–7**
(Spila Riccardo); Alamy Images pp. **22–23** (G P
Bowater); Alamy Images/AA World Travel Library
p**15** top; Alamy Images/qaphotos.com pp. **8–9**;
Corbis p. **9** inset (Roger Ressmeyer); Getty
Images/Dorling Kindersley p. **13**; Getty
Images/Photographer's Choice pp. **18–19**; Getty
Images/The Image Bank pp. **10–11**; Photolibrary.com
/Index Stock Imagery pp. **24–25**; Science Photo
Library p. **15** bot (John Heseltine), p. **14** (Jonathan
A. Meyers); Science Photo Library/British Antarctic
Survey pp. **26–27**; Science Photo Library/NOAA
pp. **4-5**.

Cover artwork of digging earth by Darren Lingard.

Illustrations by Bridge Creative Services.

The publishers would like to thank Nancy Harris and
Harold Pratt for their assistance in the preparation of
this book.

Every effort has been made to contact copyright
holders of any material reproduced in this book. Any
omissions will be rectified in subsequent printings if
notice is given to the publishers.

Disclaimer
All the Internet addresses (URLs) given in this book
were valid at the time of going to press. However,
due to the dynamic nature of the Internet, some
addresses may have changed, or sites may have
changed or ceased to exist since publication. While
the author and publishers regret any inconvenience
this may cause readers, no responsibility for any
such changes can be accepted by either the author
or the publishers.

It is recommended that adults supervise children on
the Internet.

Contents

Some words are printed in bold, **like this**. You can find out what they mean on page 30. You can also look in the box at the bottom of the page where they first appear.

Our Home Planet

Where do you live? Do you live in a city or in the desert? Do you live on an island or on a mountain? Wherever you live, your home is on **planet** Earth. A planet is a large, round body. It moves around a sun. A planet is made up of rock or gas, or both.

Earth is part of a **solar system**. Our solar system is made up of the Sun and nine planets. The Sun is at the center. All the planets move around the Sun.

Earth is the third planet from the Sun. It is not the biggest planet. It is not the smallest planet. Earth has the things we need to live. It has oxygen to breathe. It has water to drink. It has energy from the Sun for warmth and light.

Take a walk!

Imagine you could walk around Earth without stopping. It would take you almost a year to get back to where you started!

planet   large, round body that moves around a sun
solar system   sun with planets moving around it

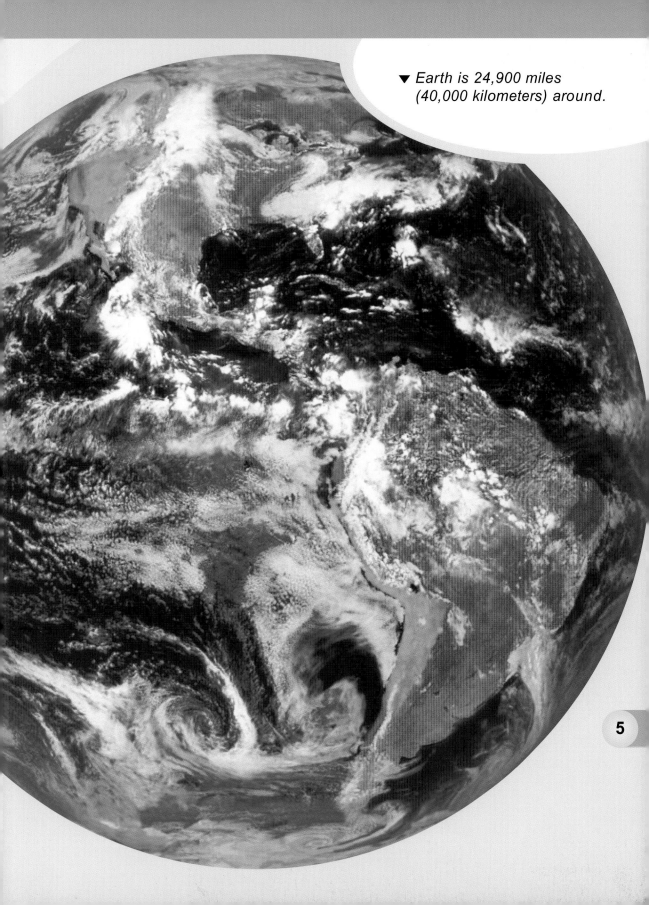

▼ Earth is 24,900 miles (40,000 kilometers) around.

5

Water covers more of ▶
the Earth than land.

minerals rocks are made of these

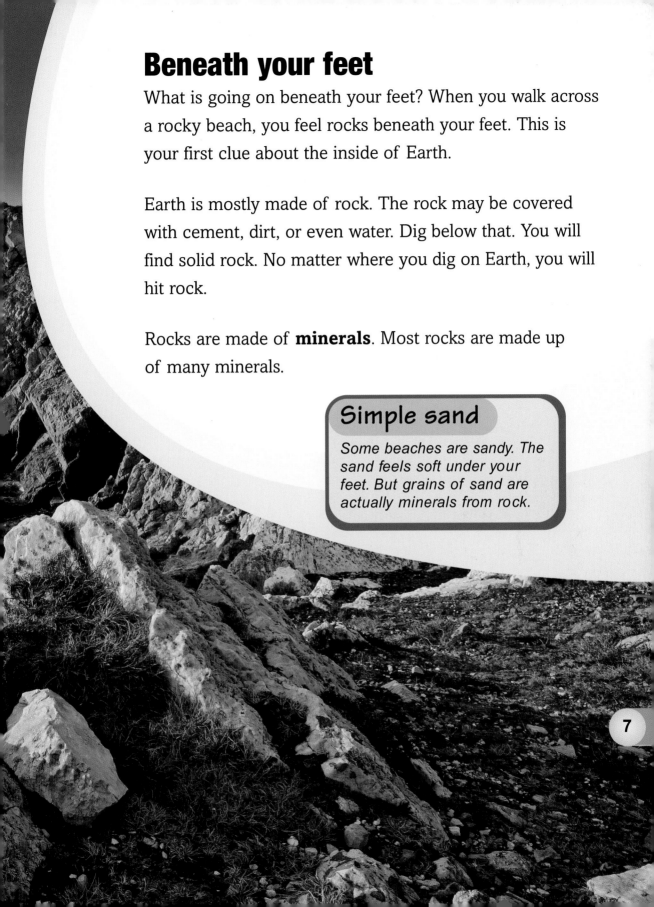

Beneath your feet

What is going on beneath your feet? When you walk across a rocky beach, you feel rocks beneath your feet. This is your first clue about the inside of Earth.

Earth is mostly made of rock. The rock may be covered with cement, dirt, or even water. Dig below that. You will find solid rock. No matter where you dig on Earth, you will hit rock.

Rocks are made of **minerals**. Most rocks are made up of many minerals.

Simple sand

Some beaches are sandy. The sand feels soft under your feet. But grains of sand are actually minerals from rock.

Earth's Center

Imagine digging down to Earth's center. The center of Earth is called the **core**. Of course, no one has ever dug to the center. Inside, the Earth is very hot. There is a lot of **pressure**. The pressure could press down and crush you. People could not survive the heat and pressure. It is not really possible to travel to the core.

This giant drill digs▶ tunnels. It can drill through solid rock.

core   center of Earth
pressure   force of something pressing down or against something else

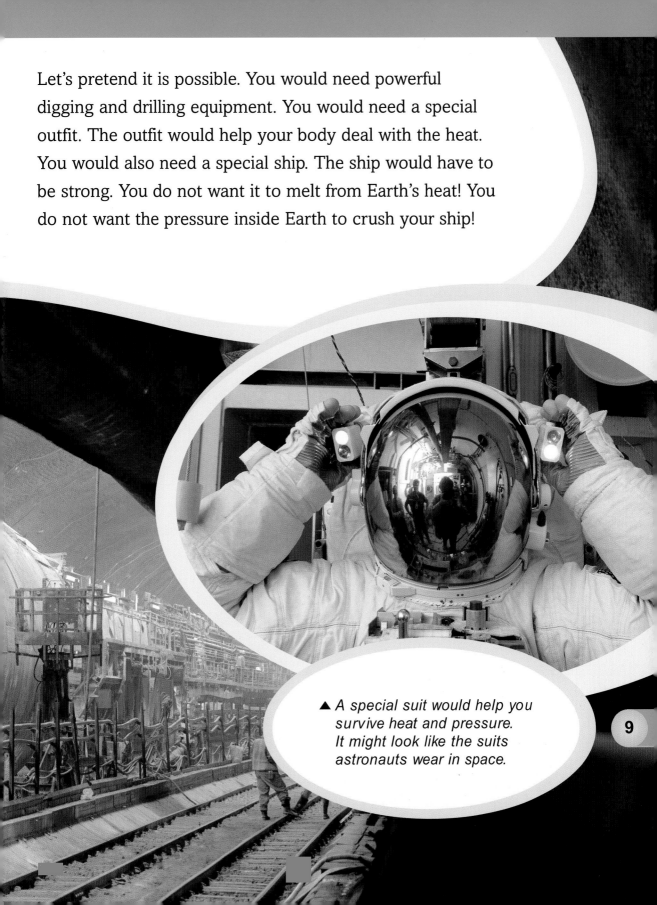

Let's pretend it is possible. You would need powerful digging and drilling equipment. You would need a special outfit. The outfit would help your body deal with the heat. You would also need a special ship. The ship would have to be strong. You do not want it to melt from Earth's heat! You do not want the pressure inside Earth to crush your ship!

▲ A special suit would help you survive heat and pressure. It might look like the suits astronauts wear in space.

Digging Deep

If you want to go to Earth's **core**, the first step is to dig a hole. By digging, you poke a hole in Earth's top layer. This top layer is made of soil.

Soil is made up of different **minerals**. Minerals are parts of rock. The minerals are all crushed up together. Soil also has **organic** matter. Organic matter is made up of pieces of dead plants and animals. Minerals and organic matter help plants grow.

In some places Earth's top layer is only a few feet (1 meter) deep. In other places it can be up to 1 mile (1.6 kilometers) deep! That may sound deep. It is very thin compared to the rest of the Earth. Digging will take you only a small part of the way toward Earth's core.

A bulldozer can dig ▶ through only the very top layer of Earth.

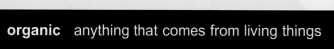

organic anything that comes from living things

First Stop: The Crust

The top layer of soil is part of Earth's outer layer. This outer layer is the **crust**. You walk on Earth's crust every day. The crust surrounds Earth. It surrounds it like an eggshell. An eggshell, though, is **fragile**. It breaks easily.

Earth's crust is very, very hard. That is because it is made of rock. You will need a powerful drill to break through the crust under the soil.

This diagram shows the ▶ layers of Earth. You can see the thickness of each layer. The top layer is the crust.

mantle

crust

Land and water

Earth's crust is not the same all the way around. The crust below the ocean is thinner than the crust below land. The crust is about 5 miles (8 kilometers) thick at its thinnest. It is about 25 miles (40 kilometers) thick at its thickest.

12

crust top, outer layer of Earth
fragile able to be broken easily

shell

◀ *Earth's crust is like the shell of an egg, but much harder!*

outer **core**

inner core

Rock groups

Let's begin drilling through Earth's **crust**. It is not easy! The crust is made of different rocks. Some rocks are not very hard. They are easy to drill through. Others are harder. They are more difficult to drill through. All of the rocks on Earth are in one of three groups.

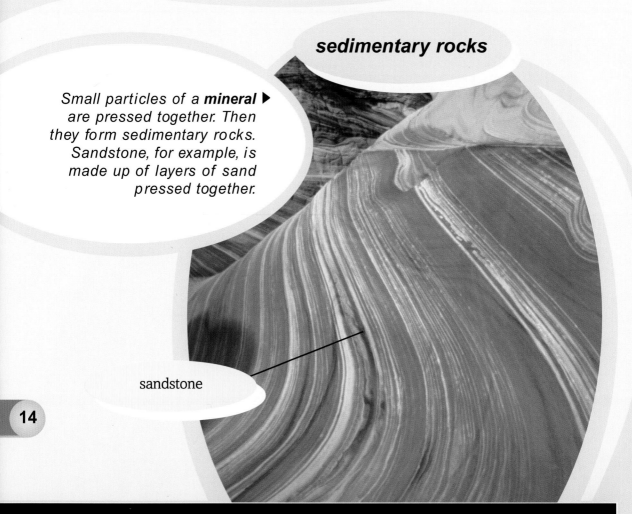

sedimentary rocks

*Small particles of a **mineral** ▶ are pressed together. Then they form sedimentary rocks. Sandstone, for example, is made up of layers of sand pressed together.*

sandstone

igneous rock	rock formed from melted minerals
metamorphic rock	rock formed from heating and cooling
sedimentary rock	rock formed from pressure pressing small particles together

igneous rocks

granite

◀ *Deep inside Earth, melted minerals cool and harden. Then they form igneous rocks.*

metamorphic rocks

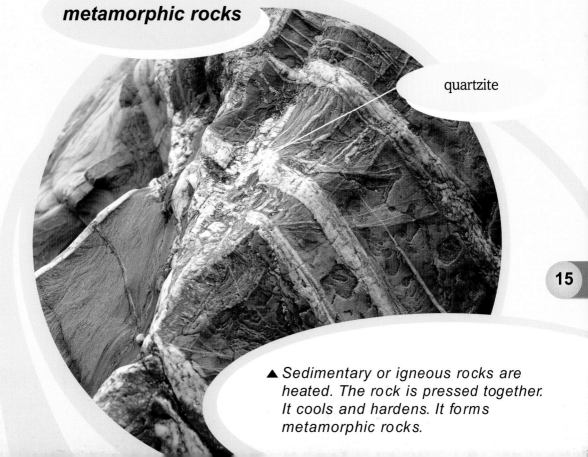

quartzite

▲ *Sedimentary or igneous rocks are heated. The rock is pressed together. It cools and hardens. It forms metamorphic rocks.*

Land on the Move

The land beneath your feet feels like it is still. But it is not still. It is always moving. Earth's **crust** is not one large solid piece. Instead, it is broken into very large sections. These sections are called **plates**.

These plates move. They float on the next layer of Earth. Sometimes the plates rub against each other. The rubbing creates heat. **Pressure** builds up. The plates slip past each other. This makes an **earthquake** happen.

Sometimes melted rock, hot ash and gases erupt onto the surface. This makes a **volcano**.

On the move

Not so long ago, scientists thought that Earth's crust was solid. They only realized it was made of moving plates in the 1960s and 1970s. Now they know that Earth used to look very different.

earthquake	shaking or trembling of Earth that may cause cracks on the surface
plate	large piece of Earth's crust
volcano	cone-shaped hill or mountain that erupts melted rock

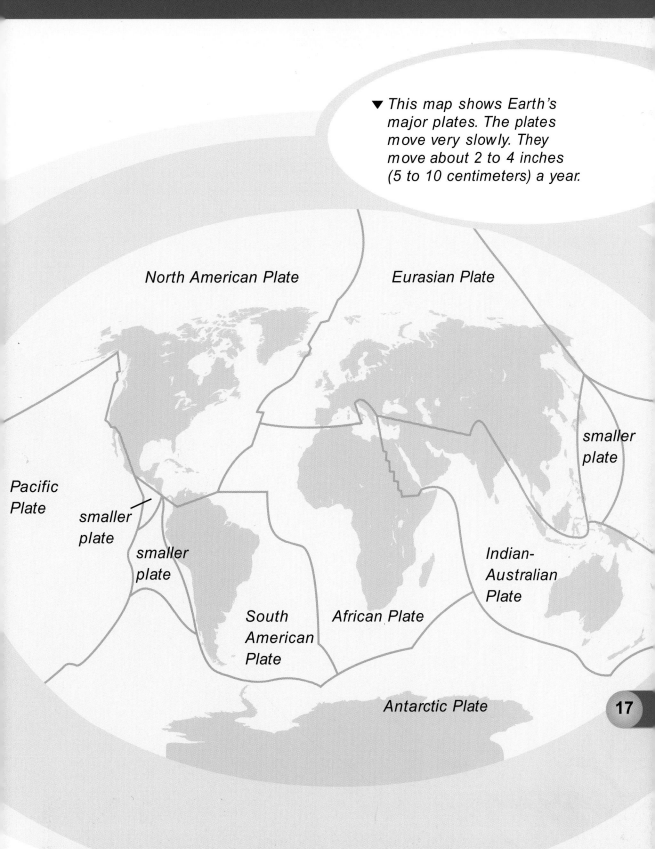

▼ *This map shows Earth's major plates. The plates move very slowly. They move about 2 to 4 inches (5 to 10 centimeters) a year.*

North American Plate

Eurasian Plate

smaller plate

Pacific Plate

smaller plate

smaller plate

Indian-Australian Plate

South American Plate

African Plate

Antarctic Plate

Next Stop: The Mantle

You have drilled through Earth's **crust**. You are about to burst through to Earth's next layer: the **mantle**. Put on your special suit! It is very hot within the mantle.

The mantle is the thickest layer of Earth. It is about 1,800 miles (3,000 kilometers) thick. The mantle is made of thick, hot rock. The rock in the mantle moves. It moves very, very slowly below the crust.

Magma

*The mantle and crust meet. In some places the heat melts the mantle. It turns the solid rock into **magma**. Magma is melted rock. It flows like honey.*

lava	hot melted rock erupted from a volcano
magma	melted rock inside Earth
mantle	layer of Earth between the crust and the outer core

▼ Have you ever seen a **volcano** erupt? Melted rock shoots out of the top of the volcano. The melted rock is called **lava**.

19

Keep going!

The **mantle** has two parts. There is an upper mantle and a lower mantle. Both parts are made of hot, slowly moving rock. The lower part is very hot. It is about 7,500 °F (4,150 °C). You will need a **protective** (safe) layer between you and the heat.

The mantle does not stay still. Hotter rocks from the lower part push their way up. These rocks force the cooler rocks above to move out of the way. Slowly, they move toward the center. Then the cooled rocks heat up, and they move up. They push the other rocks down. This causes the hot and cool rocks to move in a circle.

So slow

The movement of the mantle is very, very slow. A ship traveling through the mantle would not feel the mantle moving.

The material in the mantle is ▶ constantly moving. These arrows show the direction of movement within the mantle.

protective   able to keep you safe

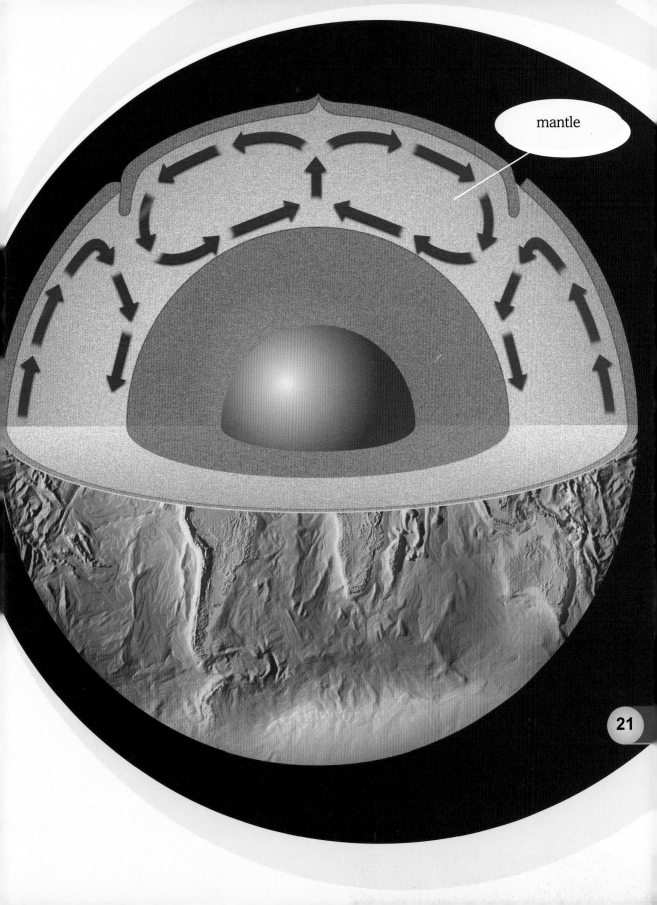

Final Stop: The Core

You made it to the **core**! But you are still not at the center of Earth. Earth's core has two parts. The first part is the outer core. It is about 1,300 miles (2,100 kilometers) thick. The outer core is not solid. It is **molten**. It is made up of very hot liquid **metal**. This liquid metal moves very slowly around the inner core.

If you could travel through the outer core, you would not need a drill. You would, however, need heat shields. These shields would need to protect you from the extreme heat. The heat in the outer core is about 9,000 °F (5,000 °C). That is hot enough to melt metal! The **pressure** is also very strong. A real ship would be crushed by the pressure. It would also be melted by the heat.

When metal becomes very hot, it ▶ melts. In the outer core, you would find melted nickel and iron. Nickel and iron are kinds of metals.

22

metal   substance such as iron
molten   melted

Inner core

Get out the drill again! You will need it to get to the very center of Earth. The very center of Earth is the inner core. The inner core is made of solid **metal**.

The very center of Earth is a solid ball of iron. Iron is a kind of metal. It would be hard to drill through the iron. The center of the Earth is also very hot. It is about 11,000 °F (6,100 °C).

The Moon is a bit larger than ▶ the Earth's inner core.

inner core

Size it up

The inner core is a little smaller than the Moon. Add the outer core. The two parts together are bigger than the Moon.

How Do They Know?

Let's head back to the surface. No one has ever really traveled to Earth's **core**. Instead scientists have figured out what the inside of Earth is like. Rocks break up in an **earthquake**. These rocks release **energy** (power). This energy travels through the Earth in waves. The waves of energy are called **seismic waves**. Scientists study seismic waves.

Seismic waves can move through rocks and liquids. They move differently through different things. For example, they travel fast through thick, hard rock. Scientists measure the speed of seismic waves. This tells them the thickness of Earth's layers.

Digging deep

*The deepest hole ever dug was about 7 miles (11 kilometers) deep. That is about a third of the way through the **crust**. The hole was dug in Russia. Scientists dug the hole to learn more about Earth's crust. It took 24 years to dig that deep. Now a team from Japan is trying to dig through to the **mantle**.*

energy   power
seismic wave   wave of energy (power) that travels through Earth

▲ Scientists examine rocks. They learn about Earth's history and layers. Scientists also look at **lava** from **volcanoes**. It tells them what is happening inside Earth.

Match the Layers

Can you remember where you have been? These flags label each layer of Earth. Match each description on the postcards with the right layer of Earth.

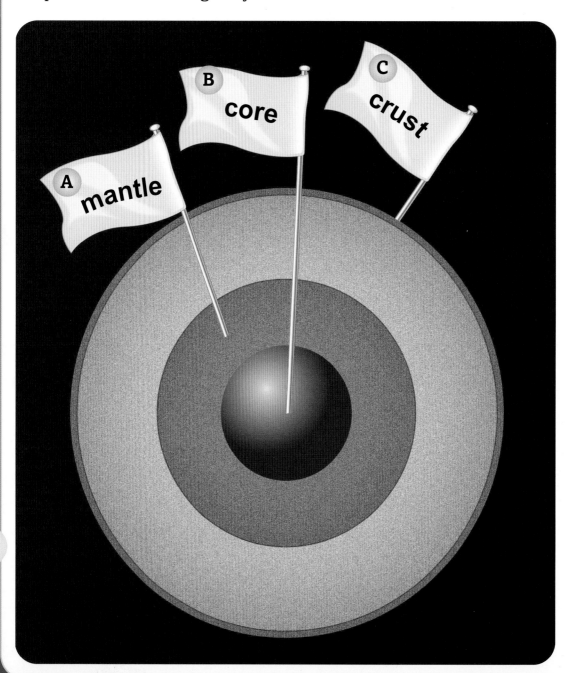

1

We had a bumpy ride through this part of Earth! The rock was thick and hot. It kept moving!

2

Whew! The deeper we went, the hotter it became. We had to drill through solid iron. The trip was not easy. But it was worth it!

3

This part of Earth is rocky. We had to drill through sedimentary rocks, metamorphic rocks, and igneous rocks. Wish you were here!

Answers: 1-A, 2-B, 3-C.

Glossary

core center of Earth. The inner core of Earth is solid iron.

crust top, outer layer of Earth. The Earth's crust contains rock and soil.

earthquake shaking or trembling of Earth that may cause cracks on the surface. Earthquakes can be dangerous.

energy power. Energy gives things the power to move.

fragile able to be broken easily. An eggshell is fragile.

igneous rock rock formed from melted minerals. Granite is a kind of igneous rock.

lava hot melted rock erupted from a volcano. Lave is magma that came from deep inside Earth.

magma melted rock inside Earth. Magma spews out as lava when a volcano erupts.

mantle layer of Earth between the crust and the outer core. The mantle is made of slowly moving rock.

metal substance such as iron. Metal can get very hot.

metamorphic rock rock formed from heating and cooling. Quartzite is a type of metamorphic rock.

minerals rocks are made of these. Sand is a mineral.

molten melted. Lava is molten rock.

organic anything that comes from living things. The Earth's crust contains organic materials.

planet large, round body that moves around a sun. We live on planet Earth.

plate large piece of Earth's crust. The movement of the plates sometimes causes an earthquake.

pressure force of something pressing down or against something else. There is a lot of pressure in Earth's core.

protective able to keep you safe. Sun cream protects you from the Sun.

sedimentary rock rock formed from pressure pressing small particles together. Sandstone is one type of sedimentary rock.

seismic wave wave of energy (power) that travels through Earth. An earthquake causes seismic waves.

solar system sun with planets moving around it. Our solar system has nine planets.

volcano cone-shaped hill or mountain that erupts melted rock. A volcano destroys homes when it erupts.

Want to Know More?

Books to read

- Harman, Rebecca. *Earth's Changing Crust: Plate Tectonics and Extreme Events.* Chicago: Heinemann Library, 2005.

- Mason, Paul. *The World's Most Dangerous Places.* Chicago: Raintree, 2006.

- Oxlade, Chris. *Rock.* Chicago: Heinemann Library, 2002.

- Whitehouse, Patricia. *The Earth.* Chicago: Heinemann Library, 2004.

Websites

- http://volcano.und.nodak.edu/ vwdocs/vwlessons/lessons/Earths_ layers/Earths_layers1.html

  Click "next" to view the next layer of Earth.

- http://scign.jpl.nasa.gov/learn/ plate1.htm

  Take a peek inside Earth.

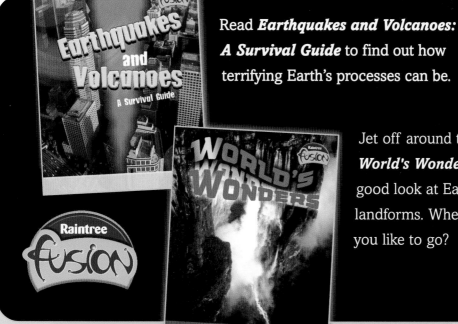

Read ***Earthquakes and Volcanoes: A Survival Guide*** to find out how terrifying Earth's processes can be.

Jet off around the world in ***World's Wonders***. Take a good look at Earth's landforms. Where would you like to go?

Index